Credit Score Optimization

Unlocking Financial Success

Table of Contents

Chapter 1. Introduction

In our Special Report, "Credit Score Optimization: Unlocking Financial Success", we delve into the profound world of financial management, breaking it down into digestible, action-oriented steps. This topic might sound technical, but we assure you, it's one we've transformed into a surprisingly accessible roadmap. With our step-by-step approach, we'll guide you on an enlightening journey, effortlessly helping you understand how to optimize your credit score. This isn't just a report - it's your key to unlocking previously out of reach financial opportunities and the life you've always envisioned. Imagine stepping into your dream car or nestling into the comfort of your first home. This report pushes you closer to those dreams. So let's navigate the complex realm of credit scores together, unraveling monetary mysteries and empowering you to grasp financial success firmly in your hands!

Chapter 2. Understanding the Basics of Credit Scores

Before diving headlong into strategies to optimize your credit score, it is imperative to understand what a credit score is, how it is calculated, and why it is so crucial in today's financial landscape. This understanding will lay the groundwork for all intricate aspects to come. Let's start by demystifying this seemingly complex term.

A credit score is a statistical number that evaluates an individual's creditworthiness based on their credit history. Lenders use credit scores to predict the potential risk associated with providing credit to a person. In theory, individuals with high credit scores are considered less risky than those with low credit scores.

But does everyone have a credit score? Yes, as long as they have a credit history with one of the major credit bureaus - Equifax, Experian, and TransUnion.

2.1. Understanding How Credit Scores Are Calculated

Understanding how your credit score is calculated is crucial for managing and improving it. Credit scoring models are multifaceted and consider various factors from your credit report.

1. Payment History (35%): Paying your bills on time is one of the most significant factors that affect your credit score. This records every payment you've ever paid late. Even one late payment can negatively impact your score.

2. Credit Utilization (30%): This measures how much of your available credit you're using; keeping this ratio low is beneficial. For example, if your combined credit limits total $10000 across

all your credit cards and you constantly have a balance of $2000, your credit utilization is 20%."

3. Length of Credit History (15%): The age of your credit accounts also matters; a longer credit history is better for your credit score. This not only includes the age of your oldest account but the average age of all your accounts.

4. New Credit (10%): Your score can come down if you've opened many credit accounts too recently. This indicates a higher level of risk to lenders, so be cautious of the frequency.

5. Credit Mix (10%): This reflects the various types of credit in use, such as credit cards, retail accounts, installment loans, vehicle loans, and a home mortgage.

As you see, a credit score does not depend on a single element, but a combination of all these factors.

2.2. The Importance of Credit Scores

Why do we need to care about credit scores? The primary reason is that a credit score plays a significant role in determining whether you'll qualify for products like insurance, mortgages, loans, and credit cards. What's more, it can also influence the interest rate you'll pay on these borrowing instruments.

Good credit isn't just about getting good rates on your loans, though that's a huge advantage. Here are a few more reasons why a good credit score is essential:

- It could help you land a job: Many employers check the credit reports of potential employees as part of the hiring process. A good credit score can, therefore, make you a more attractive candidate for a job.

- It can save you money on deposits: Utility service providers often check your credit before establishing service. A poor credit score might mean you need to pay a deposit or a higher deposit, which you can avoid with a better score.

- It can help with rental approvals: Many landlords also check the credit of potential renters. So a good credit score can help you secure that dream apartment.

As you can see, your credit score is more than just a number. It's a gateway to new opportunities and a tool for enhancing your financial stability.

2.3. Monitoring and Controlling Your Credit Score

Monitoring your credit score regularly is another key part of understanding the credit scoring system. Regular monitoring can help you know where you stand and take control of your financial health.

Various companies provide free credit reports from the three major credit bureaus once every year. Take advantage of these offers and check your credit reports for mistakes, as errors can lower your credit score. If you notice any inaccuracies, it's crucial to dispute them and have them removed from your report.

Maintaining a higher credit score is no mystery. It involves the basics of sound financial health – timely payment of bills, not getting into unnecessary debt, and keeping a low balance on your credit cards. It isn't about never borrowing money, but rather managing that borrowed money responsibly.

By now, you should have a basic understanding of what a credit score is, how it's calculated, and why it's essential. But we're just getting started. In the following chapters, we'll explore more on how to optimize your credit score, delve into the factors that impact your credit score the most, and how to influence each one positively.

Buckle up; we're embarking on a journey towards better financial health!

Chapter 3. The Impact of Credit History on Your Score

Your credit score is a three-digit number that comes from the information in your credit report. It tells lenders how likely you are to pay back a loan on time. A high score can help you qualify for the best loans and conditions, while a low score can make it more difficult. Your credit history, or the record of how you've managed borrowed money in the past, plays a crucial role in determining this score.

3.1. The Relationship Between Credit History and Your Credit Score

Lenders want to know your financial past to predict your future behavior. This is why your credit history holds significant importance. Let's discuss how a history of credit impacts your credit score.

When determining your credit score, the credit bureau considers several factors: your payment history, amount of debt, length of credit history, new credit, and your credit mix. Each carries a different weight in the overall score, and some reflect your credit history more than others.

3.1.1. Payment History

The most influential factor in your credit score is your payment history, making up approximately 35% of your overall score. This metric looks at your record of paying back loans and credit cards on time. Late payments, defaults, and bankruptcies have a significant negative impact on your score.

Your payment history also includes public records such as bankruptcy, tax liens, or civil judgments. These significant negative events remain on your credit report for seven to ten years, but their impact on your score decreases over time. However, a good payment history can alleviate any previously damaging activities.

3.1.2. Amount Owed

The amount you owe accounts for nearly 30% of your credit score. Lenders are interested in how much existing debt you have, how many accounts you owe money on, and how much of your available credit you're using, also known as your credit utilization ratio. Keeping low balances on credit cards and other credit accounts can lead to a higher credit score.

3.1.3. Length of Credit History

The length of your credit history contributes approximately 15% to your credit score. Your credit history length is measured from your oldest account and the average age of all your accounts. Lenders prefer to see a long history of good credit management, as it provides more information about your behaviour as a borrower. Shopping for credit too frequently can shorten your average credit age, potentially lowering your score.

3.1.4. New Credit and Credit Mix

Other factors that impact your credit score include any new credit, which constitutes about 10% of your score, and your credit mix or types of credit accounts you have such as credit cards, auto loans, mortgages, which makes up another 10%.

If you frequently open new accounts, lenders may view you as more risky, potentially resulting in a lower credit score. Demonstrating responsibility with a variety of credit types can improve your score, but it's not a good idea to open accounts you don't intend to use.

3.2. How to Improve Your Credit History

Improving or maintaining your credit history is vital for optimizing your credit score. Here are some tips to ensure a healthy credit history:

1. Pay your bills on time: Your payment history is the biggest factor affecting your credit history, so it's crucial to pay all your bills promptly.

2. Keep your balances low: Your credit utilization rate also plays a significant role. The smaller the percentage of available credit you're using, the better your score will be.

3. Don't close old accounts: Keeping long-standing accounts open and active can add history and depth to your credit history.

4. Diversify your credit types: Having a mix of credit types can show lenders you're capable of managing different kinds of credit effectively.

5. Limit your applications for new credit: Each time you apply for credit, a hard inquiry is created on your credit report, which can lower your credit score.

In conclusion, your credit history shapes your credit score. By taking control of your credit and learning how to leverage it responsibly, you can enjoy the benefits that come from having a higher credit score - such as lower interest rates, faster loan approvals, and access to better financial opportunities.

Chapter 4. Credit Utilization and Its Role in Credit Scoring

Credit scores are a calculated measure, a numerical way for lenders to understand your creditworthiness. The higher your credit score, the more confident a lender will be in extending you credit. But what is it that builds this score? While there are many factors, a prominent one is your credit utilization. This ratio directly impacts your credit score significantly, and understanding its role can help you master the art of financial success.

4.1. Understanding Credit Utilization

Credit utilization can seem a complex term at first glance, but it's quite simple. It refers to the percentage of your available credit that you are currently using. It is calculated by dividing the total amount you owe by the total credit limit available to you. For example, if you have a total credit limit of $10,000, and you're using $2,500 of that, your credit utilization ratio is 25 percent.

A lower credit utilization ratio signals creditworthiness to lenders, as it shows you manage your credit well and you're not over-reliant on borrowed resources. On the other hand, a high ratio indicates potential financial stress, which can negatively impact your credit score.

4.2. The Impact of Credit Utilization on Your Credit Score

The crucial interface between credit scores and credit utilization occurs because it serves as an indicator of your financial health.

Credit utilization accounts for approximately 30% of your FICO score, the most commonly used credit score model. This makes it the second most critical factor after payment history.

A high utilization rate may signify that you are over-dependent on debt, increasing the perceived risk to lenders. This increased risk can lower your credit score, potentially limiting your access to future credit or resulting in higher interest rates.

Conversely, a low utilization ratio implies you manage your debts effectively, are less reliant on credit, and are thus a lower risk to lenders. Therefore, maintaining a lower ratio can positively affect your credit score.

4.3. How to Calculate Credit Utilization

Calculating your credit utilization is a simple, straightforward task. As mentioned previously, you simply need to divide your total credit card balances by your total credit card limits. It's worth noting that this ratio is typically calculated on both a per-card and overall basis.

If you have multiple credit cards, the overall credit utilization ratio will present a more accurate idea of your credit usage. This is simply the sum of the balances of all your credit cards divided by the sum of the limits of all your credit cards.

4.4. Ways to Manage Credit Utilization

Knowing that credit utilization significantly impacts your credit score, you must consciously manage it to maintain a healthy credit profile.

- Pay Your Balances in Full Each Month: **Paying your balances in full each month is an effective strategy, as it reduces your credit utilization ratio before it's reported to the credit bureaus.**

- Increase Your Credit Limits: Another method to lower your credit utilization ratio is to request a credit limit increase on your credit cards. Use this added availability responsibly; don't take it as an invitation to spend more.

- Apply for Additional Credit: You may also choose to apply for a new credit card to increase your total available credit, subsequently lowering your utilization ratio. However, this strategy should be pursued judiciously, as applying for too much credit in a short time can negatively affect your credit score.

- Consider Balance Transfers: If a single card has a high utilization rate, it may be worth considering a balance transfer to a card with a lower utilization ratio. This helps even out the distribution of your balances.

- Monitor Your Ratios Regularly: Regular monitoring of your credit utilization ratios can help you stay on top of any rising balances and take swift action.

4.5. The 30% Rule of Credit Utilization

A widely accepted rule within financial circles is to maintain a credit utilization ratio below 30 percent. Although the scoring models don't officially recognize this figure, it is a good benchmark to follow for a healthy credit profile.

This 30% rule, also known as the Credit Utilization Rule, suggests that using more than 30 percent of your available credit limit may signal financial stress to a lender, potentially diminishing creditworthiness in the eyes of lending institutions.

Balancing your credit utilization is not a once-and-done task. It requires continuous effort, timely check-ins, and tweaks based on your credit behavior. However, managing this carefully can help position you favorably to lenders, boosting your credit score and opening doors to the financial opportunities you desire. Hop aboard the journey of financial success with a keen eye on your credit utilization. With this article, you now have the tools to better manage this key factor, widening the pathway to the quality of life you've always envisioned.

In conclusion, your credit utilization ratio is a powerful lever you have over your financial destiny. Through effective management, you can transform this seemingly esoteric financial concept into a tangible stepping stone towards brighter and more secure financial horizons. In your hands lies the key to lowering your ratio, enhancing your credit score, and unlocking the door to financial success.

Chapter 5. The Importance of Payment History in Your Credit Score

The formula that equates to your credit score may be complex, but certain elements carry more weight than others. One such significant factor is your payment history, which constitutes approximately 35% of your FICO Score. It sets the bedrock of your credit profile. Let's venture deep within it and comprehend its nuances and importance.

5.1. Understanding Payment History

Your payment history is, in simpler terms, a record of your paying habits. Every time you make payment against your credit card, auto loan, student loan, mortgage or any other form of credit extended to you, it is recorded for reference.

Lenders use it to gauge your reliability. They perceive the borrowers who make payments on time as less likely to default. Thus, your payment history provides an essential predicting element for creditors while deciding whether to extend their credit facility to you.

If you've consistently made your payments on time, your history radiates a strong image portraying you as a reliable borrower. However, if you've missed payments, made late payments, or have defaults and bankruptcies recorded in your credit history, it signals lenders that lending to you might carry a potential risk.

5.2. The Correlation Between Payment History & Credit Score

Understanding the direct correlation between your payment history and credit score is crucial. It fundamentally forms the largest portion of your credit score calculation for a reason: to depict your financial behavior. Evidence of punctual payments suggests you manage your credit responsibly, while late payments, defaulted loans and bankruptcies can indicate a lack of fiscal discipline.

Included in your payment history are:

- Payment information on various types of accounts (credit cards, retail accounts, installment loans, finance company accounts, mortgage, etc.)

- The presence of adverse public records (bankruptcy, suit judgments, liens, wage attachments, etc.), collection items, and/or delinquency (past due items)

- Severity of delinquency (how long past due)

- Amount past due on delinquent accounts or collection items

- Time since past due items (delinquency) and public records or collections

5.3. Impact of Late Payments on Your Credit Score

Late payments can severely dent your credit score. Even a single delayed payment can lead to a drop of several points in your score, and the ill-effects amplify with the severity, frequency, and recency.

The direct correlation of late payments and credit score is complex and varies. In general, the higher your credit score, the more it gets impacted by the late payment.

Additionally, the later the payment, the more it hurts your credit score. Payment that is 60 or 90 days late will have a more significant impact than a payment that is 30 days late.

It's also important to remember that the effect of a late payment on your credit score diminishes over time. Keeping up with your payments will gradually improve your credit score.

5.4. Repairing Blemishes in Your Payment History

The detrimental effects of these slips-ups, however, can be repaired over time. Derogatory marks on your credit report stay there for a while - late payments can typically stay for seven years, and bankruptcies can remain for up to ten years.

But keep in mind, the impact of these financial hiccups gradually decreases over time. The freshness of your credit habits is critical to lenders. Thus, if you start making consistent, on-time payments, your credit score will incrementally improve. This indicates you've taken control of your finances, and modified your habits, which will positively impact future lending decisions.

When trying to repair your payment history, consider the following steps:

1. Budget wisely: This will help ensure timely payments of all your dues.

2. Set up automatic payments: This will help avoid forgetting due dates.

3. Aim to repay more than your minimum obligation: This aids in reducing your overall debt faster and could help boost your credit score.

4. Communicate with your lenders: If you're struggling with making payments, talk to your lenders about possible solutions or payment plans.

5.5. The Road Ahead

By understanding the core aspects of payment history and its importance in constructing your credit assessment, you're a step closer to optimal financial planning - always aim to make timely payments, be mindful of the amount of debt you accumulate, and remember to enable this habit as a consistent practice. Your efforts will be duly rewarded with a robust credit score, opening up multiple avenues in your financial journey.

In summary, nurture good credit habits, rectify past missteps, and keep moving forward. After all, your credit score is not just a number—it's a reflection of your financial health and discipline, and it carries meaningful implications for your future financial success. Putting in the effort to optimize your score can pay off generously, yielding dividends in terms of better loan offers, lower interest rates, and unlocked financial opportunities.

Chapter 6. How Credit Inquiries Can Affect Your Credit Score

It's vital to understand that when you apply for credit, the lender will evaluate your creditworthiness. This process involves a credit inquiry — a review of your credit report by a lender. Credit inquiries can—and often do—impact your credit score. But how severely and how long they'll affect it can vary. Let's delve into the nuances of credit inquiries.

6.1. The Two Types of Credit Inquiries

There are two types of credit inquiries: hard inquiries and soft inquiries. Each caters to different needs and affects your credit score differently.

Hard inquiries, also known as 'hard pulls', occur when you apply for a loan, credit card or mortgage, and the lender checks your credit report to decide whether you're a safe credit risk. These inquiries can have an impact on your credit score.

On the other hand, soft inquiries, or 'soft pulls', occur when a person or company checks your credit report as part of a background check. This might happen, for example, when a credit card issuer checks your credit without your application to decide whether you qualify for certain credit card offers. Soft inquiries do not impact your credit score.

6.2. Impact of Hard Inquiries

Each hard inquiry on your credit report could deduct five to ten points from your credit score. However, the impact on your credit score diminishes over time. Hard inquiries only remain on your credit report for two years. After that, they disappear and no longer affect your score.

It's also noteworthy that although each hard inquiry may slightly lower your credit score, multiple inquiries for the same type of loan within a specified timeframe (usually between 14-45 days) are typically treated as a single inquiry. This is because most scoring models understand that you are rate shopping and therefore they don't penalize you for it.

6.3. Frequency Matters

Yet, if you apply frequently for new credit over a short period, it can signal to lenders that you are financially stressed or overly dependent on credit, which can make you appear riskier. A flood of hard inquiries could convey financial desperation to potential lenders, who may then be hesitant to offer you credit terms on account of perceived risk.

6.4. Mitigating The Impact

Few strategies can help you soften the blow of hard inquiries. First and foremost: apply for new credit only when necessary. Carefully ponder over whether you can afford a new line of credit, keeping potential interest charges and fees in mind.

Second, do your rate shopping within a condensed period. Since credit scoring models typically count multiple hard inquiries for the same type of loan as one if done within a 14-45 day period. By doing this, you ensure that you don't unknowingly damage your credit score through multiple hard inquiries.

6.5. Inquiries vs. Credit Mix

While it's essential to be cautious of the number of hard credit inquiries on your report, keep in mind that this is only a small portion of your overall credit score. Credit inquiries influence just 10% of your FICO Score. It's ways better to focus on paying your bills on time and reducing your credit utilization - those two categories alone contribute to 65% of your FICO Score.

When it comes to maintaining and optimizing your credit score, it's all about balance. You need a mix of credit types - like credit cards, retail accounts, installment loans, finance company accounts, and mortgage loans - to demonstrate that you can manage all types of credit responsibly.

6.6. Conclusion

Understanding the ins and outs of credit inquiries and their effects on your credit score will help you achieve optimal financial health. While credit inquiries are important, focusing on the factors with greater weight, such as payment history and credit utilization, is vital too. Managing these aspects skillfully will get you closer to achieving your financial goals. Remember, knowledge is power, and gaining insights into the intricacies of your credit score will help you wield this power wisely.

Chapter 7. Strategies for Debt Management to Optimize Credit Score

Financial success often hinges upon your ability to manage and control your debts. Countless individuals struggle to climb out of the debt-hole due to mismanagement and lack of knowledge. However, with the right strategies, you can keep your debts under check, bolster your credit score, and unlock doors to your financial dreams.

7.1. Understanding Your Debt

Before diving into debt management strategies, let's begin with comprehending the full extent of your debt. Note down all your liabilities, including personal loans, credit card debts, student loans, mortgages, etc. Use a simple table like so:

```
|=======
| Debt | Amount | Interest Rate | Repayment Priority |
|-------|---------|------------------
|----------------------|
|Credit card| $5,000 | 15%|High|
|Student loan| $20,000| 6.8%|Medium|
|Personal loan| $2,000| 9%|High|
|Mortgage| $200,000| 3.6%|Low|
|=======
```

This table will offer you a clear picture of your debt landscape. The repayment priority typically depends on interest rates, with higher rates necessitating quicker repayment.

7.2. Implement a Budget

Drawing up a precise budget is the first real step towards successful debt management. To create a budget, follow these steps:

1. Write down your income sources and their corresponding amounts.

2. Compile all your expenses.

3. Deduct your expenses from your income to grasp your disposable income.

4. Dedicate a portion of your disposable income for repaying debts.

5. Ensure that you have a small stash for savings, even if it's minimal.

Keep your budget realistic, flexible, and adaptable to keep up with changes in your income or expenditures.

7.3. Debt Snowball and Avalanche Methods

When managing your debts, two popular strategies are the debt snowball and avalanche methods.

The debt snowball method advocates paying off the smallest debt first (irrespective of the interest rates). This serves to motivate you by providing quick wins.

The avalanche method argues for paying off your highest interest rate debt first, which saves more money in the long run.

Opt for the strategy you find most motivating and sustainable.

7.4. Prioritize High-interest Debt

High-interest debts can quickly drain your resources. Therefore, it's imperative you address these first. This includes payday loans or credit card debts, which commonly sport high interest rates.

By prioritizing high-interest debts, you'll save on interest payments and clear your obligations faster.

7.5. Seek Lower Interest Rates

Do not hesitate to request lower interest rates from your credit card companies or any other lenders. Even a single percentage point reduction can make a significant difference, especially for larger debts.

For instance, if you have a good repayment record, your credit card company might agree to reduce your interest rate. Alternatively, you could consider transferring your balance to a card with lower rates.

7.6. Consolidate Your Debts

Debt consolidation refers to combining your debts into a single loan with a lower interest rate. It can simplify your repayments and replace your high-interest debts with a more manageable one.

However, tread cautiously with debt consolidation. The long-term implications need to be considered and understood.

7.7. Negotiate Your Debt

Negotiating your debts directly with creditors isn't always successful, but it is a viable strategy. You could negotiate reduced interest rates, extended pay-off periods, or even a reduced total amount owed.

7.8. Automate Repayments

Automating debt repayments helps you avoid missed payments, which can lead to penalties and reported delinquencies to credit bureaus. Consistent, timely repayments are vital in maintaining and improving your credit score.

7.9. Avoid New Debt

While paying off existing debt, barring necessities such as a mortgage, refrain from making significant new purchases on credit. Acquiring new high-interest debts will only put you back in the debt pit.

In conclusion, debt management boils down to structured, disciplined steps aimed at reducing and ultimately eliminating your debts. By understanding, measuring, and addressing your debts strategically, you can optimize your credit score. Remember, patience is key here, as improving your credit score is a marathon, not a sprint. Your financial freedom and success are worth the time and dedication required on this journey.

Chapter 8. The Role of Credit Mix in Credit Score Enhancement

If you want to enhance your credit score, understanding the concept of a "credit mix" is undeniably important. Essentially, the term refers to the different types of credit you currently hold. This may range from credit cards and auto loans to home mortgages or student loans. Remarkably, credit mix accounts for 10% of your FICO Score, one of the most popular credit scoring models that lenders use.

8.1. Importance of Credit Mix

While payment history and amounts owed - the first and second critical factors - are rather intuitive when it comes to their impact on credit scores, the importance of credit mix may not immediately seem obvious.

Expanding your credit mix, i.e., maintaining diverse types of credit, indicates your ability to efficiently manage varied types of debts. Lenders and credit bureaus evaluate this to gauge how reliable you'd be in repaying future debts. Recognizing this pivotal role of credit mix in credit score enhancement can effectively steer your financial management strategies.

Remember, however, that credit mix impacts only a fraction, 10%, of your FICO score. It won't be a magic wand to spectacularly boost your credit overnight. Nonetheless, all the components of a credit score interact with each other, with none operating in isolation. For instance, maintaining a diverse credit portfolio but defaulting on payments would likely harm rather than help your score. This interconnectivity is another crucial reason to understand the broader context when focusing on credit mix.

8.2. The Components of Credit Mix

To strengthen your credit mix, you first need to identify its components. They generally fall into two primary categories: revolving credit and installment credits.

While revolving credit includes credit cards and home equity lines, the installment credit list embraces car loans, mortgages, and student loans.

Revolving Credit: This is a more flexible kind of credit. Here, you're provided with a credit limit, and you can choose how much to borrow each month. The credit card is the classic example.

Installment Credit: This is a type of credit wherein a specific loan amount is borrowed, and that loan is repaid with interest in equal periodic payments.

Both types of credit have different attributes and add unique value to your credit mix.

8.3. Diversify Your Credit Mix

Getting diverse types of credit often indicates to creditors that you're able to manage all your credit responsibly, which might increase your creditworthiness. And there's evidence in FICO's data that borrowers with a good mix of credit tend to be less risky.

A good strategy to diversify your credit mix could involve responsibly managing different forms of credit. For instance, taking out a small auto loan, if repaid regularly, can boost your credit score over time.

Remember that this doesn't mean you should go out and secure every type of loan available - that would be detrimental. The key is to manage a variety of credit types effectively and responsibly over time.

8.4. Optimize, Don't Maximize Credit Types

Just because a diverse credit mix can improve your credit score doesn't mean you need to go out and open one of each type of account. Instead, you should aim to gradually build a diverse history of well-managed credit.

One strategy could involve starting with a secure credit card where you must deposit money upfront as a collateral. These cards are easier to acquire for individuals with a thin credit history or lower credit score. As you accumulate on-time payments through this card, you may qualify for an unsecured credit card.

Aim to maintain low credit utilization, ideally less than 30% of your limit, across all cards. After establishing a strong credit card repayment history, consider adding a low-interest installment loan, such as an auto or personal loan, to your portfolio.

8.5. Credit Mix: Part of a Bigger Picture

Finally, it's important to remember that while credit mix is a significant factor, it's just a single piece of a larger puzzle. Creditors look at many factors to determine your creditworthiness.

In fact, the two most influential factors are your payment history and amounts owed, which collectively make up 65% of your FICO Score. Thus, it's critical to keep up with all loan payments and strive to decrease credit utilization, irrespective of your credit mix.

In conclusion, mastering your credit mix is a strategic way to enhance your credit score, but it must be done responsibly. Optimize your credit types, foster a diverse credit history without maximizing credit, and always remember the interplay between different credit score components. By doing so, you'll slowly but surely pave the way toward an excellent credit score. By mastering this puzzle piece, you'll gain greater control over your financial future.

Chapter 9. Rebuilding Credit Scores: Hope after Financial Setbacks

Rebuilding credit is like rebuilding a house after a storm. It requires time, patience, and the appropriate tools. But with diligent and consistent efforts, it is indeed possible to recreate a solid structure of financial credibility that lenders will trust. Let's begin our journey together with the four critical pillars to your credit rebuilding process – Understanding the Credit System, Developing a Strategy, Implementing Your Plan, and Tracking Your Progress.

9.1. Understanding the Credit System

Before undertaking any rebuilding project, it's crucial to comprehend the blueprint. When it comes to credit scores, you need to understand the factors that influenced your score in the first place.

There are five main elements:

- Payment History (35%): This is your track record of how timely you have repaid any loans or credit card dues.

- Credit Utilization (30%): This refers to the percentage of your available credit that you're currently using.

- Length of Credit History (15%): The age of your oldest and newest credit accounts, including an average age of all your accounts.

- Credit Mix (10%): The types of credit you have, which could include credit cards, retail accounts, installment loans, finance company accounts, and mortgage loans.

- New Credit (10%): The number of new accounts you've opened or applied for recently, including the number of hard inquiries lenders made when you applied for credit.

Understanding these factors is the cornerstone of building a solid and effective credit repair strategy. The more you understand these, the better equipped you are to take control of your financial future.

9.2. Developing a Strategy

Once you've comprehended the credit system's intricacies, it's time to develop a personalized repair strategy.

Here are some fundamental steps to craft your custom plan:

1. Obtain a areport of your credit score: You're entitled to one free report per year from each of the three major credit reporting agencies, namely Experian, Equifax, and TransUnion. Get these reports and study them well.

2. Identify negative items: Look for any entries that led to a decrease in your score. It may include late payments, bankruptcies, collections, or hard inquiries.

3. Dispute errors: If you notice any discrepancies, raise a dispute with the credit bureau reporting the erroneous information. Provide them with any documents to support your case.

4. Pay off your debt: Create a realistic budget that prioritizes paying down existing debt, starting with the highest interest balances first.

9.3. Implementing Your Plan

After devising your personalized credit repair strategy, it's time to put the wheels in motion. Here are four key steps to begin implementing your plan:

1. Establish a timely payment routine: This step cannot be overstated. Prompt payments contribute significantly to your credit score. Even if you can only afford minimum payments initially, always pay on time.

2. Limit your spending: Live within, or preferably below, your means. Ideally, you should be using only 30% of your available credit limit.

3. Diversify your credit: If possible, try to have different types of credit on your report, like a mix of a credit card, retail account, and installment loan.

4. Avoid new debt: Keep hard inquiries to a minimum. Each time a prospective lender checks your credit; it can slightly lower your credit score.

5. Seek professional help: If your financial situation is complicated, considering seeking advice from a credit counseling agency.

9.4. Tracking Your Progress

Remember, rebuilding credit is not an overnight process. It requires constant monitoring and adjustments to your strategy where necessary.

1. Keep checking your credit score: Many credit card providers now offer free access to credit scores on their online platforms. Regularly track your progress and adjust your strategy accordingly.

2. Sign up for credit monitoring services: Several free and fee-based services are available that will allow you to monitor your credit progress.

3. Seek professional advice: If you are unsure or overwhelmed, never hesitate to seek assistance from credit counseling agencies. They can provide insights, recommendations, and resources to help boost your credit restoration journey.

Rebuilding credit after significant setbacks can seem like a formidable journey. However, with a solid understanding of the principles that govern credit scores, a dynamic and tailored strategy, rigorous implementation of your plan, and ongoing monitoring of your progress, it is indeed possible to reconstruct your financial credibility. Remember, slow and steady wins the race in credit recovery. Take it one small step at a time, and before you know it, you'll find yourself closer to your financial goals than ever before.

Chapter 10. Credit Score Myths Busted: Separating Fact from Fiction

Credit score myths often mislead individuals, obscuring their understanding and preventing them from unveiling the full potential of their personal finances. This confusion can hinder your ability to optimize your credit score, slowing your journey towards financial success. This section aims to dispel these wide spread fallacies, proving them wrong one by one, so let's get started.

10.1. MYTH 1: Checking Your Credit Hurts Your Score

One of the pervasive myths you might have come across is that checking your credit score will lower it. This belief stems from a misunderstanding of a 'hard inquiry' and a 'soft inquiry'. A hard inquiry is initiated by potential lenders or credit card companies when you apply for credit, and this might have a small, temporary impact on your score. On the other hand, a soft inquiry is when you or a company checks your credit score or when a credit card company pre-approves you for a promotion, and it does not affect your credit score. So, keep yourself informed about your credit score, it's a pivotal element of financial growth and an integral part of this guide.

10.2. MYTH 2: You Only Have One Credit Score

It's a widespread assumption that individuals only possess a single credit score. However, this couldn't be further from the truth.

Consumers, in fact, have multiple credit scores generated by different credit reporting agencies such as Experian, Equifax, and TransUnion. Each of these agencies might have information that the others don't, resulting in variations in the scores. Additionally, different financial institutions use different models to calculate credit scores, such as VantageScore and FICO.

10.3. MYTH 3: Closing Old Credit Cards Boost Your Credit Score

Closing old credit cards, contrary to popular belief, does not improve your credit score. It might even harm it. Closing a credit card can decrease your overall credit limit, thereby increasing the utilization rate, a key factor affecting your credit score. A lower utilization rate, i.e., a lower ratio of credit used to the total credit limit, is beneficial for your score. Therefore, rather than closing old credit cards, aim to keep them active and balance your credit usage intelligently.

10.4. MYTH 4: Age Doesn't Affect Credit Score

Age itself doesn't affect your credit score, but the age of your credit history does. The length of your credit history accounts for about 15% of your FICO Score. A longer credit history provides more data and, consequently, a better prediction of credit behavior. It's beneficial to start building your credit history early, but remember, it's never too late to start.

10.5. MYTH 5: You Need to Carry a Credit Card Balance to Improve Credit Score

There exists a common misconception that suggests carrying a balance on your credit card can lead to an improved credit score. This is untrue. In fact, carrying a balance may increase your credit utilization ratio, which can be detrimental. Paying your balance in full each month, conversely, doesn't harm your credit score.

10.6. MYTH 6: All Debt Is the Same

Not all types of debt are weighed equally. Credit scoring models distinguish between the types of debt- revolving (credit card) and installment loans (mortgage). Credit mix, the types of debt you have, accounts for 10% of your FICO score. A mix of both installment and revolving credit can improve your credit score, but it's not essential to have both types. Always remember, regardless of the type, it's pivotal to fulfill all credit obligations on time.

In conclusion, the myths surrounding credit scores unfortunately saturate discussions surrounding financial management. Understanding the facts and not falling prey to these misconceptions can create a substantial difference in credit score optimization, paving your way towards financial success. Refer to this portion if you find yourself entangled in these myths and use this understanding as a tool to debunk them, taking control of your journey towards financial literacy and prosperity. This was a step forward in our exploration into the universe of credit scores and the influential role they play in our financial canvas. Grasp these facts and stride ahead into the empowering world of financial success.

Chapter 11. Advanced Strategies for Sustaining High Credit Scores

The journey to achieving high credit scores requires careful planning, deliberate action and a deep understanding of how credit systems work. But once there, a different kind of challenge arises – maintaining and sustaining these scores. This section provides an advanced approach to handle this task, with strategies tailored to individuals who have already laid strong credit foundations.

11.1. Understanding the Importance of Sustaining High Credit Scores

Even though you've reached a comforting credit score, you must understand one critical fact: credit scores are not static. They can rise and fall with your actions, inactions, rough economic cycles, or unexpected life events. A high credit score unlocks a wide range of financial opportunities – from lower interest rates to superior credit card benefits. But these benefits can easily be lost if not properly managed.

11.2. Continuous Monitoring and Regular Credit Report Reviews

Regular reviews and monitoring are essential steps in sustaining high credit scores. They help you to stay abreast of any changes in your credit score, acting as a routine health check.

1. Obtain your credit report from each of the big three credit bureaus – Experian, Equifax, and TransUnion – on an annual

basis.

2. Diligently review your credit reports for any errors that could affect your scores—things like incorrect balances, false delinquencies, or fraudulent accounts.

3. If disputes arise, challenge such errors immediately to maintain your credit's health.

11.3. Possessing Diverse Types of Credit

Having different types of credit in your credit history plays a pivotal role in maintaining high credit scores. It gives lenders a broader perspective on how you manage various types of debt.

1. Maintain a healthy mix of credit such as retail accounts, installment loans, credit cards, and a mortgage.

2. Remember not to open unnecessary credit accounts solely to increase your credit mix, as this could lead to overspending and affect your overall credit score.

11.4. Low Credit Utilization Rate Maintenance

Credit utilization rate – the percentage of your total available credit in use – carries substantial weight in your credit score calculation.

1. Strive to keep your credit utilization at or below 30%. A lower rate shows lenders you're not heavily reliant on credit and manage it responsibly.

2. Regularly review your credit card statements to ensure you're not creeping up on your credit limit.

11.5. On-Time Payments and Debt Management

Even at the stage of high credit scores, your payment history proves critical.

1. Aim to make all payments on time – from credit card bills to utilities and other monthly commitments.

2. Should you find it tough to keep track of various bills, automate your payments whenever possible.

11.6. Managing Credit Applications

Every time you apply for new credit, your credit report records a hard inquiry.

1. Minimize external credit applications as repeated hard inquiries can negatively impact your score.

2. Apply for new credit only when necessary. Each application might seem insignificant, but they add up over time and could harm your high credit score.

As you can see, no magic formula maintains high credit scores. It's more about continued fiscal discipline, awareness, and intentional strategies to manage your credit effectively. You've mastered the basics of obtaining a high credit score, and advanced strategies for sustaining it are just an extension of what you've already been practicing. Stay diligent, remain informed, and continue regulating your financial activities, always aware of how they affect your credit scores. By doing so, you're solidifying your financial future.